KNIGHT

READY FOR BATTLE

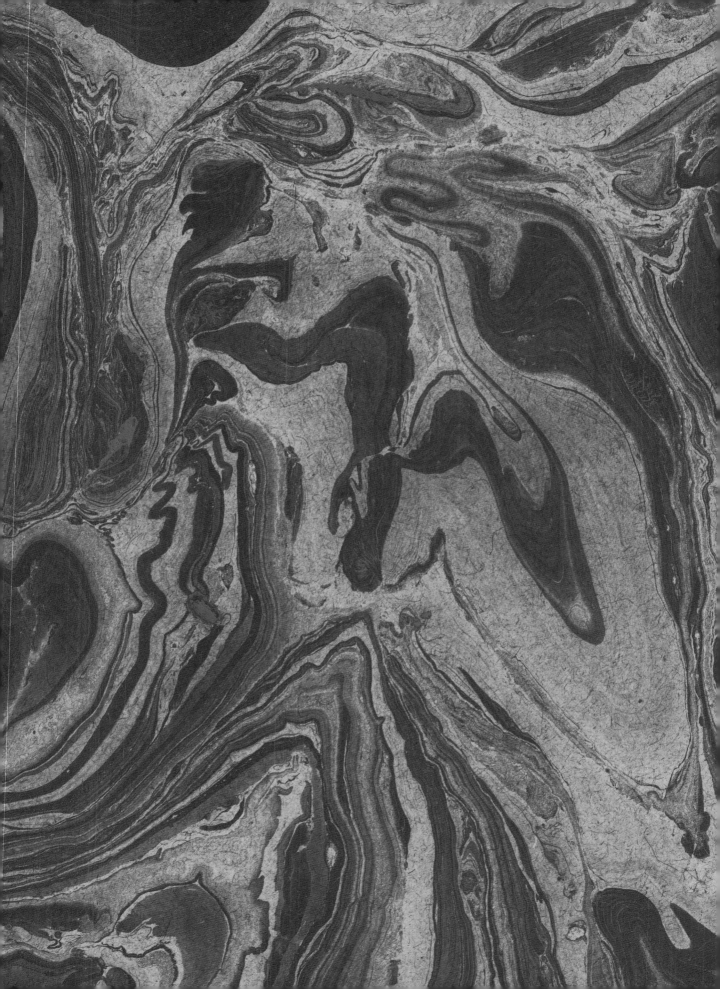

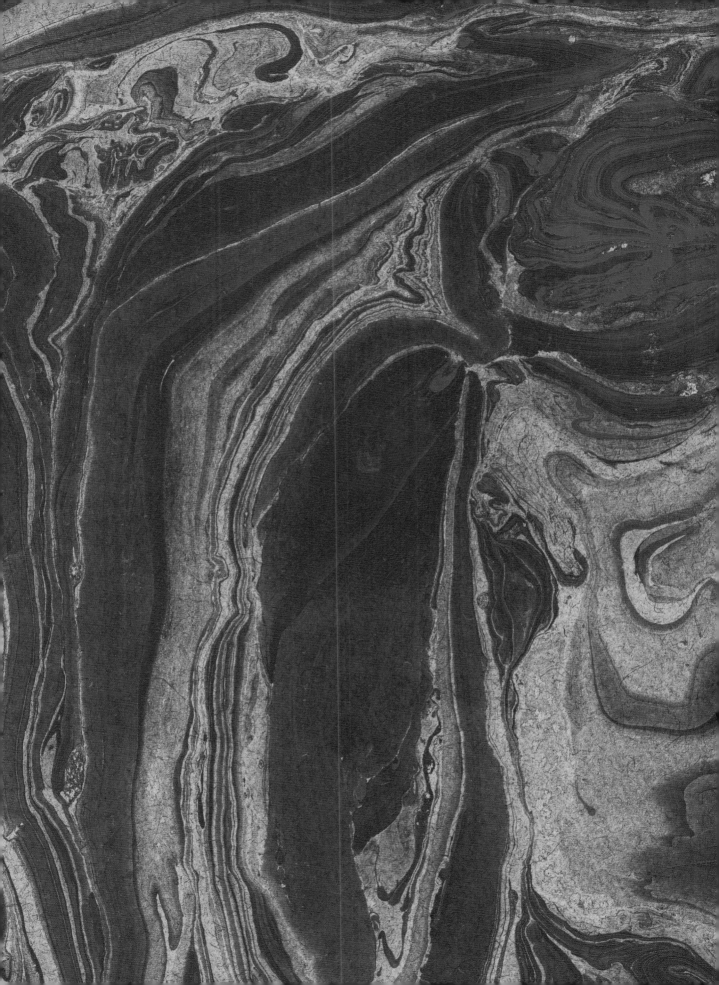

Contents

Published by **S** SCRIBO
25 Marlborough Place, Brighton BN1 1UB
A division of Book House, an imprint of
The Salariya Book Company Ltd
www.salariya.com
www.book-house.co.uk

S A L A R I Y A

1 3 5 7 9 8 6 4 2

A CIP catalogue record for this book is available
from the British Library.

Printed and bound in China.
Printed on paper from sustainable sources.

PB ISBN-13: 978-1-910706-01-5

Created and designed by: David Salariya
Editor: Stephen Haynes
Editorial Assistants: Rob Walker, Mark Williams
Additional Illustrators: David Antram, Corinne and Ray Burrows, Carolyn Franklin, John James, Mark Peppé

Visit our web site at **www.book-house.co.uk**
for **free** electronic versions of:
You Wouldn't Want to be an Egyptian Mummy!
You Wouldn't Want to be a Roman Gladiator!
Avoid Joining Shackleton's Polar Expedition!
Avoid Sailing on a 19th-Century Whaling Ship!

Knight

READY FOR BATTLE

David Stewart

Illustrated by Mark Bergin

Introduction

Travel back in time to medieval Europe, between 1000 and 1500 CE. That is when knights built castles, took part in jousts and tournaments, enjoyed hunting and feasting, and fought and died in wars. This period is known as the Middle Ages, because it comes between ancient times and modern times. In the Middle Ages, land was the key to power and wealth—and the land was controlled from the castle. The most powerful person in the land was the king. He allowed nobles to hold land; in return, they promised to fight for him. The nobles in turn gave parts of their land to other knights who agreed to fight for them.

Knights had to swear an oath to be loyal to the king.

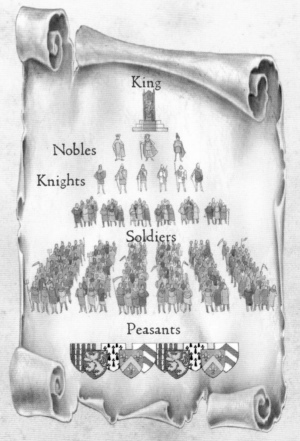

King

Nobles

Knights

Soldiers

Peasants

The King's word was law. If he wanted to, he could have you thrown into jail or even beheaded.

2

What is a knight?

Knights were not just soldiers—they were the elite fighting men of their time. Ordinary soldiers went on foot and fought with pikes and bows. Knights rode on horseback, wore high-quality armor, and used swords and lances. The equipment and the training were very expensive, so usually only boys from well-off families could hope to become knights.

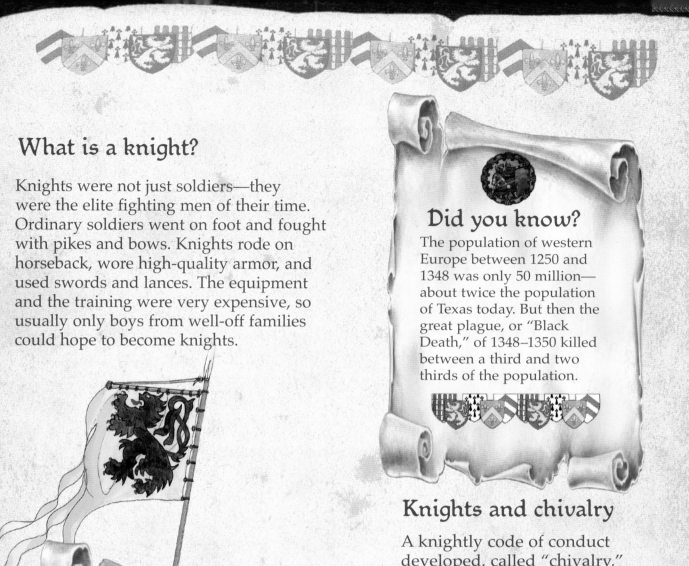

Did you know?

The population of western Europe between 1250 and 1348 was only 50 million—about twice the population of Texas today. But then the great plague, or "Black Death," of 1348–1350 killed between a third and two thirds of the population.

Knights and chivalry

A knightly code of conduct developed, called "chivalry," with an emphasis on good manners, especially toward women. Knights were expected to be honorable and brave, and to protect the weak.

Did you know?

Chivalry
The word "chivalry" originally meant that you were good on a horse. It comes from *cheval*, the French word for "horse." Later, it came to mean polite, honorable behaviour.

Training for Knighthood

The boy who was to become a knight was usually of noble birth. At the age of 7, a knight's son was sent to the castle of a great lord to become a page. There he learned how to behave, and was taught the manners of a noble. At 14, if he had done well as a page, he was made into an esquire (or squire); this was the personal servant of a knight. His duties were to look after the knight's armor, weapons, and other possessions. The esquire also accompanied the knight on campaign and helped him into his armor before battle. In return, the boy was taught the skills of a fighting man.

Usually the boy who was going to be trained to be a knight came from a wealthy family.

Education

The boy had to be able to read and write. He was taught by a monk.

The duties of a page

The page had to serve food at table.

Did you know?

The word "esquire" originally meant "shield carrier." Later it came to mean a gentleman who owned land. It comes from the Old French word for "shield," *escu*.

Training

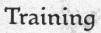

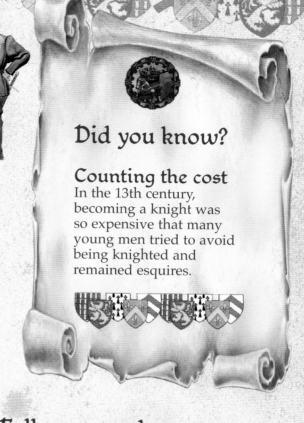

At the age of 14, when the page had become an esquire, he started to learn fighting techniques.

Quintain

When training with a quintain, the esquire had to hit the target shield then duck quickly, or the swinging weight would knock him off his horse.

Did you know?

Counting the cost
In the 13th century, becoming a knight was so expensive that many young men tried to avoid being knighted and remained esquires.

Did you know?

Wax casts
If an armorer lived a long distance away, a knight might send wax casts of his legs, arms, or torso for new armor to be fitted around.

Light weight
Some suits of armor were light enough for the wearer to be able to run in them, or even do a somersault.

Fully armored

A knight was dressed in his armor by his esquire.

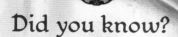

Becoming a Knight

The esquire could hope to become a knight at about the age of 21, once he had successfully completed his training. The night before he was to be knighted, the young esquire was bathed and shaved. Other esquires dressed him in special robes, and he spent the night in prayer. His nighttime vigil over, the young esquire put on his best clothes. His family and friends were waiting in the great hall of the castle, where the ceremony of dubbing would take place.

Coat of arms

A coat of arms was useful for identifying knights in a tournament or in war (see pages 14–15).

Knight school

Wooden swords were used at first to practice sword-fighting.

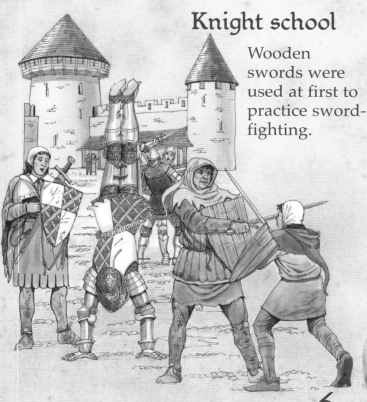

Did you know?

The Knights Hospitalers were also monks who looked after the sick. They were founded in Jerusalem in the 11th century to look after Christian pilgrims.

Did you know?

The Templars
The Knights Templars were originally formed to protect Christian pilgrims who visited the Middle East. During the Crusades the Hospitalers and the Templars fought against the Saracens.

Bathing

Water was heated on a fire and poured into a wooden tub.

The knight's vigil

The young esquire was expected to pray all night for guidance on how to be a good knight.

The ceremony of dubbing a knight

The young esquire knelt before his king or lord, who tapped him on the neck with a sword. This tapping was called an accolade. He was then given his own sword and spurs. This marked his new status as a "gentle, worthy, faithful, and devoted knight," sworn to defend churches, orphans, widows, and "servants of God." The newly dubbed knight then returned to the chapel for a blessing by a priest. The details of the ceremony varied from place to place.

Armor and Weapons

A. Gauntlet
B. Buckles and hinges

Italian knight, 1385

A knight's fighting equipment— which consisted of a sword, a shield, a suit of armor, and a warhorse—was very expensive. Altogether it might cost as much as five farm workers would be paid over twenty years. Well-made armor was almost indestructible; if it was damaged, dents could be hammered out, or broken links of mail repaired.

The pattern on this shield is called a bend raguly. (See page 14 for more examples of shield patterns.) Sometimes a small round shield called a buckler was used instead.

Arming the knight

It took about an hour for an esquire to dress a knight in his complete suit of armor.

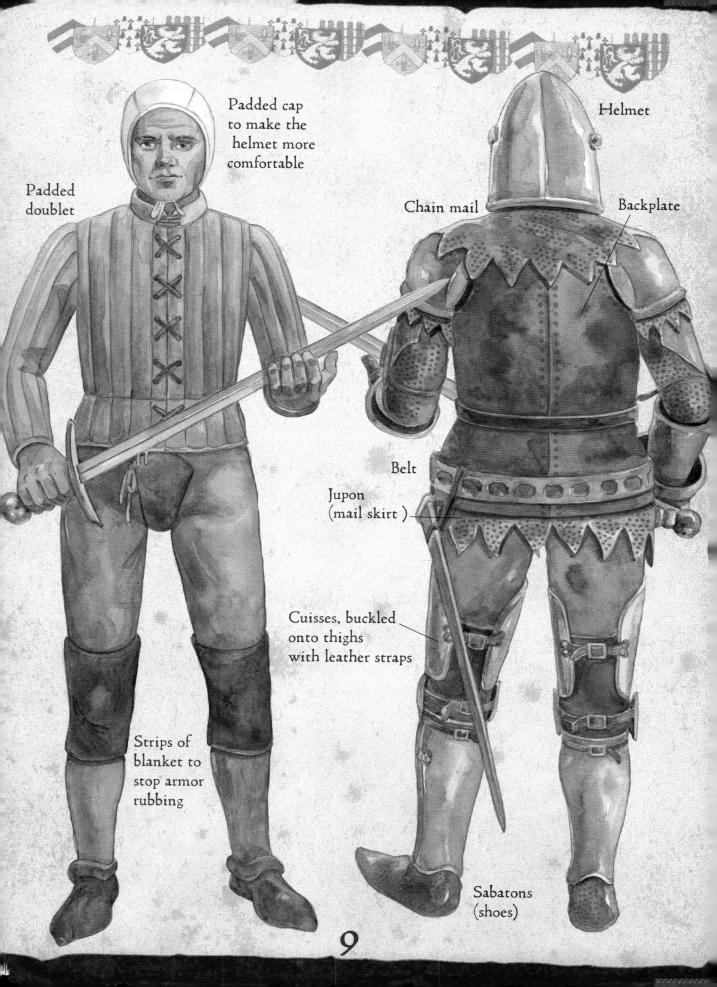

Padded cap
to make the
helmet more
comfortable

Helmet

Padded
doublet

Chain mail

Backplate

Belt

Jupon
(mail skirt)

Cuisses, buckled
onto thighs
with leather straps

Strips of
blanket to
stop armor
rubbing

Sabatons
(shoes)

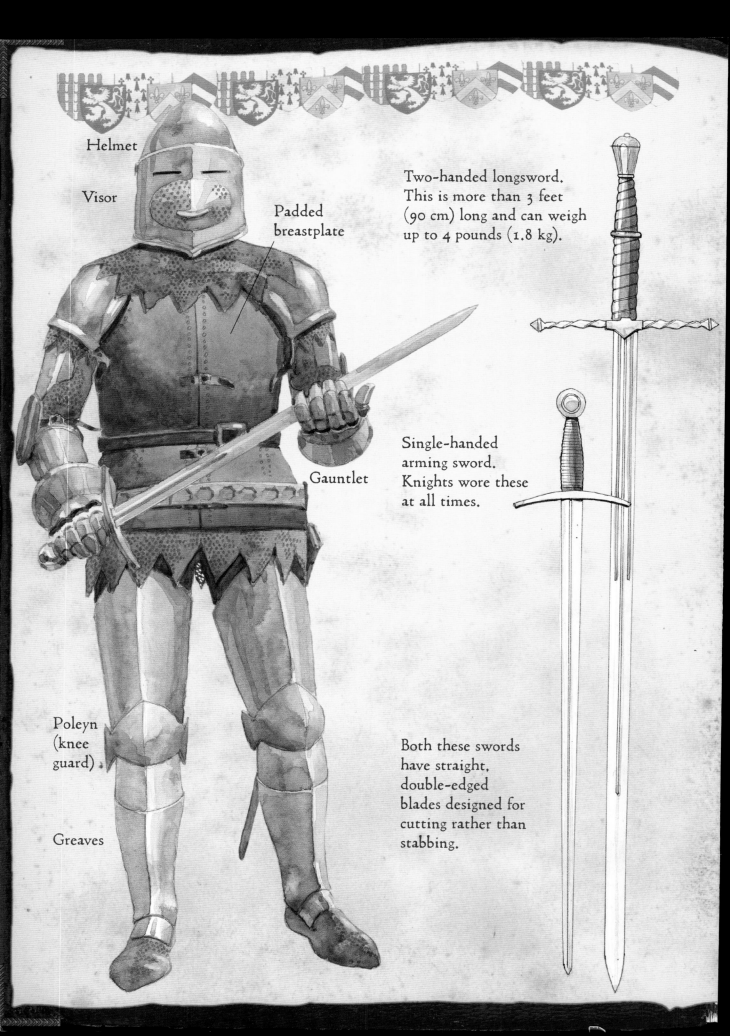

Helmet

Visor

Padded
breastplate

Two-handed longsword.
This is more than 3 feet
(90 cm) long and can weigh
up to 4 pounds (1.8 kg).

Single-handed
arming sword.
Knights wore these
at all times.

Gauntlet

Poleyn
(knee
guard)

Greaves

Both these swords
have straight,
double-edged
blades designed for
cutting rather than
stabbing.

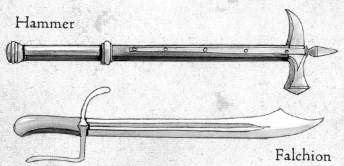

Hammer

Falchion

Wearing armor

Strong steel plate armor (white armor) weighed about 55 pounds (25 kg) and was cleverly jointed to allow the knight to move around easily. Once inside his armor, the knight was uncomfortably hot.

Armor-piercing weapons

Even the best armor could not guarantee a knight's safety. A sword could cut through a man's helmet and skull. A mace or a hammer could smash his brains out.

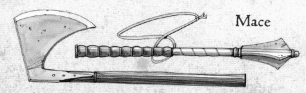

Mace

Battle-ax

Making armor

Plate armor was usually worn over a shirt of chain mail. Chain mail was made by riveting circles of wire together into interlocking rings. Armor was made by a number of different craftsmen: hammerers, mailmakers, millmen (polishers), locksmiths (who attached the hinges), and engravers and etchers (who decorated the armor with patterns).

Forging a sword

Riveting chain mail

Did you know?

Naming the parts
Every part of a suit of armor has a special name. Many of these names are French, because French was the language of chivalry. The pictures show the names of some of the most important parts.

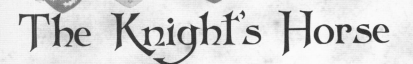

The Knight's Horse

Bridle

Rein

Bit

Breast strap

Medieval warfare depended on two main classes of fighting men: knights mounted on horseback and foot soldiers. A knight would need horses for warfare, jousting, hunting, and traveling. His most expensive horse would be his destrier or warhorse. This was a stallion. Horses to be used in battle had to be well trained. They had to get used to the smell of blood and the noise of battle.

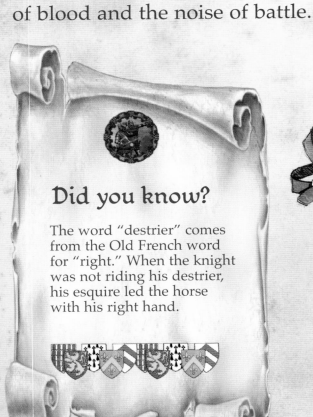

Did you know?

The word "destrier" comes from the Old French word for "right." When the knight was not riding his destrier, his esquire led the horse with his right hand.

Spurs

Iron shoe

Mail hood

Pauldron

Vambrace

Couter

Pommel

Cantle

Crupper

Spur

Scabbard or sheath

Girth

Stirrup

The right horse for the job

By the thirteenth century, knights usually had at least two warhorses: a courser and a destrier. The courser was a swift hunting horse; the destrier was used for jousting. For traveling, knights and ladies preferred more gentle horses called palfreys. Packhorses, known as sumpter horses, were used to carry baggage.

The pommel and cantle of the saddle make it difficult for the knight to be knocked off his horse.

Gilded spurs were a badge of honor, awarded for an act of bravery.

The spiked wheel at the back of the spur is called a *rowel*.

Heraldry

Checky

In the heat of battle, when knights were encased from top to toe in armor, how could you see who your friends or enemies were? It became especially difficult after the introduction of the closed helmet, which hid a man's face. A system of badges developed, called heraldry. The idea may have come from the Saracens; certainly badges began to be used during the Crusades. Designs known as coats of arms were painted on shields, and later sewn onto the knight's surcoat (a cloth garment worn on top of the armor) and horse trappings.

To begin with, only lords and knights had coats of arms. At first each knight had his own design, but later they became hereditary badges to be handed down in the family.

Chief embattled

Per pale indented

Cross engrailed

Pale

Chief

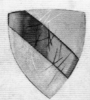
Bend

Cross

Per fesse

Per saltire

Per cross

Per pale

Paly

Barry

Dividing the shield

The basic shield shape can be divided in many different ways, each of which has its own name. Here are some of the most important designs.

The language of heraldry

Each part of the shield has its own special name:

Chief (top)

Dexter (right side)*

Sinister (left side)*

Field (background colour)

Charge (design)

* The dexter side is on the right-hand side of the knight holding the shield—when you look at the shield from the front, it looks like the left side.

Heraldic colors

The colors used on a coat of arms are called tinctures. They include two metals—argent (silver/white) and or (gold/yellow)—and five main tinctures: azure (blue, from the Arabic name for the precious stone lapis lazuli), gules (red), purpure (purple), sable (black, named from the fur of the sable marten), and vert (green).

The shield shown above has a gold lion rearing up on its hind legs, on a red background. The correct heraldic description for this design is: gules, a lion rampant or.

Impaling arms

Impaling is the joining of two coats of arms side by side in one shield. Usually this is to indicate the union of a husband and wife, with the husband's arms placed to the sinister and the wife's arms to the dexter side.

Wife's arms   Husband's arms

An example of impaled arms

Did you know?

Heraldry is still used today. European schools, stores, and companies can have their own coats of arms. In some countries there are officials—called "heralds" or "kings of arms"—to control the use of them.

Jousts and Tournaments

Tournaments probably started in the 11th century as a practice for war. Two teams of knights fought a mock battle, called a mêlée. Defeated knights could lose their horses and armor, so great fortunes could be won or lost.

Jousting

In the 13th century, jousts were added to the tournament. In the joust, knights fought on a one-to-one basis. Two knights would charge at one another at great speed and try to knock each other off their horses.

Eventually tournaments became more peaceful, with more jousting and parading than actual fighting.

A school for combat

The 12th-century crusader and historian Roger of Hoveden said:

"A knight cannot shine in war if he has not prepared for it in tournaments. He must have seen his own blood flow, have had his teeth crackle under the blow of his adversary..."

A tournament might last for several days, and at night there would be feasting—for those who were still fit!

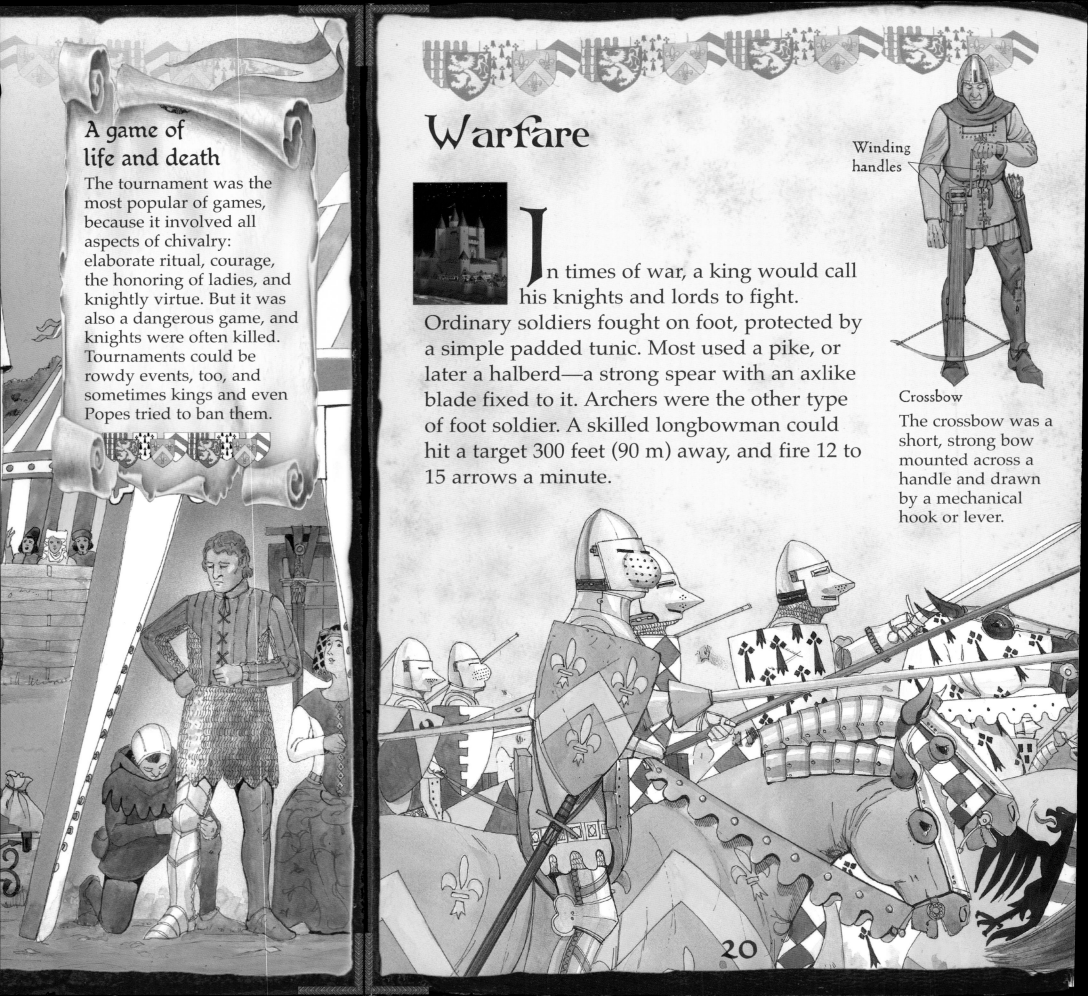

A game of life and death

The tournament was the most popular of games, because it involved all aspects of chivalry: elaborate ritual, courage, the honoring of ladies, and knightly virtue. But it was also a dangerous game, and knights were often killed. Tournaments could be rowdy events, too, and sometimes kings and even Popes tried to ban them.

Warfare

In times of war, a king would call his knights and lords to fight. Ordinary soldiers fought on foot, protected by a simple padded tunic. Most used a pike, or later a halberd—a strong spear with an axlike blade fixed to it. Archers were the other type of foot soldier. A skilled longbowman could hit a target 300 feet (90 m) away, and fire 12 to 15 arrows a minute.

Winding handles

Crossbow
The crossbow was a short, strong bow mounted across a handle and drawn by a mechanical hook or lever.

20

Winning battles

Battles were won by knights and archers fighting together in an intelligent plan. Much was at stake: defeat might mean the loss of an army, or a crown. The enemy foot soldiers would not be any match for a fully armored knight charging.

Losing battles

Ordinary soldiers captured by the enemy might be killed or deliberately maimed as a warning to others. Knights, however, were usually taken alive and held for ransom. All knights thought of other knights as equals, who deserved to be treated in a chivalrous way.

Did you know?

There was a kind of arrow that could go right through a knight's armor. The slim "bodkin" arrowheads could pierce mail and kill horses at over 300 feet (90 m). Closer up, they punched straight through plate armor.

The Crusades

Siege of Antioch, 1098

In 1071 the Seljuk Turks conquered much of the Byzantine Empire. Fearing that they might conquer Europe, Pope Urban II called for a Christian army to capture Jerusalem. The Church thought that a "holy war" would be a good way of keeping warlike knights occupied. At this time there were two different men claiming to be Pope. Organizing a crusade would give Urban an advantage over his rival.

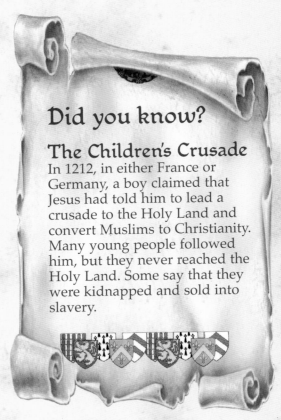

Did you know?

The Children's Crusade
In 1212, in either France or Germany, a boy claimed that Jesus had told him to lead a crusade to the Holy Land and convert Muslims to Christianity. Many young people followed him, but they never reached the Holy Land. Some say that they were kidnapped and sold into slavery.

This is how a European artist imagined Jerusalem in the 15th century.

Why Jerusalem?

Jerusalem is important to Christians, Muslims, and Jews. Christians believe that Jesus preached there and died there on the Cross. Muslims honor Jerusalem as the place where the Prophet Muhammad received a revelation of Heaven. For Jewish people, Jerusalem is the site of their holiest temple, and their traditional home. From 750 CE it had been controlled by Muslim rulers based in Baghdad, in present-day Iraq. For centuries they had allowed Jews and Christians to live there alongside Muslim citizens, but now the Christians felt that this was not enough.

Fighting top

Castle

In 1095, 4,000 knights and 26,000 foot soldiers set out from Constantinople (now Istanbul), the capital of the Byzantine Empire. After a three-year campaign they captured Jerusalem on July 15, 1099. The city of Acre, the last Christian stronghold in the Middle East, finally fell to the Muslims in 1291.

Crusaders wore the sign of the cross because they believed that fighting for the Holy Land was a Christian duty. Their cloth surcoats prevented their armor from getting too hot in the blazing sun.

What knights brought back from the Arab world

The Crusades caused death and destruction on a huge scale. But they also created a new source of wealth: They opened up trade routes to the east for merchants from Genoa, Marseille, and Barcelona. Cloth from Italy, as well as spices, silks, and cottons from Asia, enriched ports and inland towns.

The Muslim countries were famous for science and scholarship. From Muslim scholars, Europeans learned a great deal of medical knowledge and the modern system of "Arabic" numbers, including the use of zero. They also brought back many new fruits and vegetables, sugarcane and cotton, paper, many scientific devices, and new ways of working steel and leather.

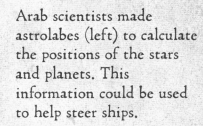

Arab scientists made astrolabes (left) to calculate the positions of the stars and planets. This information could be used to help steer ships.

Muslim scholars at work in a well-stocked library

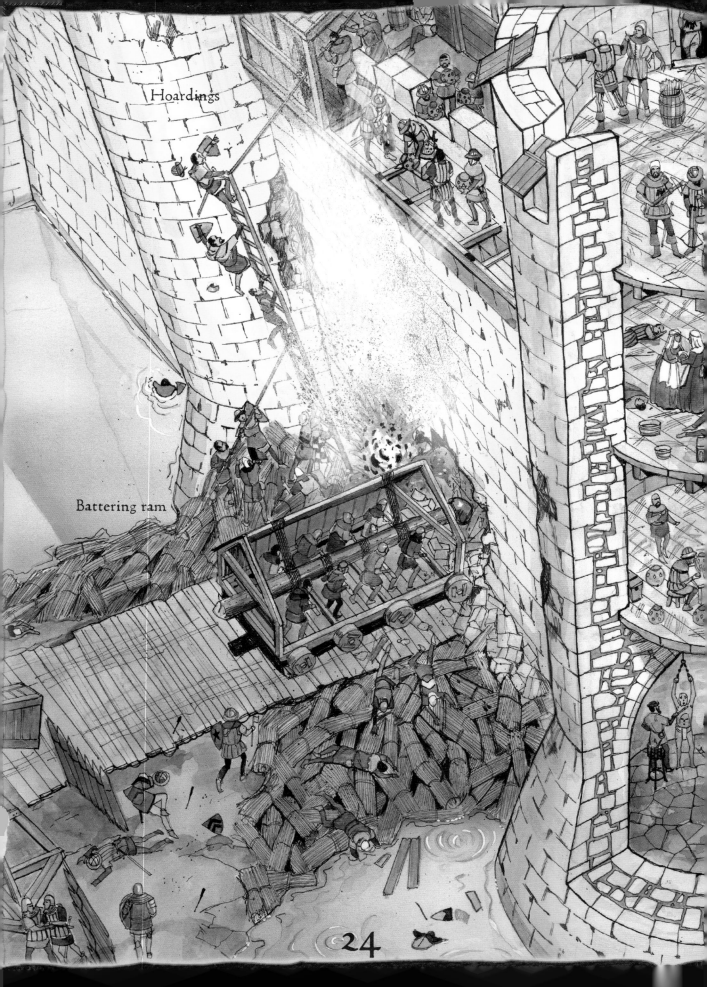

Hoardings

Battering ram

24

Under Siege

The safest way to attack a castle was by laying siege to it. The castle was entirely surrounded by troops so that supplies could not be brought in, and messengers could not get out to fetch help.

On arrival, the attackers would make a formal demand for the castle to surrender. If the defenders accepted, they were allowed to leave unharmed. If they refused, the attackers would prepare to starve them into submission.

Defenders built wooden shelters called "hoardings," which overhung the walls so that they could drop missiles on the attackers below. The pavis or pavise was a large wooden shield used by archers.

Pavise

Trebuchet

I Spy

Can you find these?

A workshop making fire pots (bombs)
Fire pots being dropped
A prisoner being tortured
Women tending the wounded
Crossbowmen winding their bows
A ladder for scaling the walls
A battery of guns

Under Siege

Siege towers and battering rams were often covered with wet animal hides, which offered some protection against fire and arrows.

Mangonel

I n the attackers' camp there would be plenty to be done. Massive siege weapons had to be assembled on the spot from parts brought in by wagon. Among them were the mangonel and trebuchet for hurling stones and boulders, the ballista for firing enormous crossbow bolts, and the siege tower for archers to fire from. Meanwhile, swords would have to be sharpened, arrows prepared, and longbows strung.

If a castle couldn't be taken by force and the defenders could not drive the enemy army away, the siege might drag on for many weeks or months. With the surrounding town and country stripped of food, the defenders of the castle could be driven to eating anything: rats, mice, grass, dogs, or tree bark. They might even cut up strips of leather and boil the hide till it was soft and chewable.

Occasionally, the siege engines might fire dead animals into the castle to spread germs. Even human heads could be used.

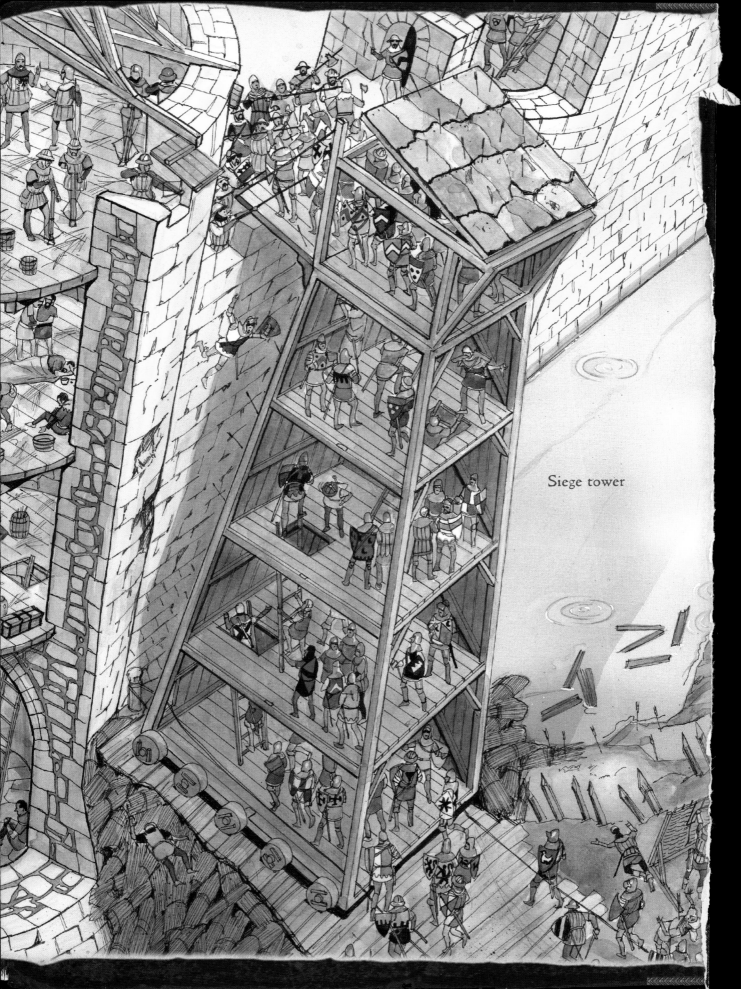

Siege tower

The Castle

A castle is a fortress built for defense against enemy armies. It was also the home of a lord and his followers. People who lived on the castle lands were also protected.

Keep

Curtain wall

Inner ward

Did you know?

Garderobe was the medieval term for a toilet, draining into a moat or ditch. It was also used as a wardrobe. Moths would stay away from the clothes because of the putrid smells wafting up from the drains.

The inner ward

The defensive walls around the castle were up to 10 feet (3 m) thick and made from two layers of masonry. The "inner ward" within them provided living quarters for servants. Chickens and pigs were kept here to provide a welcome source of fresh food. This would be particularly valuable if the castle was under siege.

Built to last

The early motte and bailey castles were gradually rebuilt in stone. The central keep was protected by an outer "curtain" wall with towers spaced along it.

Did you know?

Motte and bailey

Early castles consisted of a wooden tower built on an artificial mound or **motte**. The outbuildings are surrounded by a strong fence; the outer enclosure is called a **bailey**.

Motte and bailey castle, c.1080

The Great Hall

T he heart of the castle was the great hall. Here everyone dined together, and the lord would entertain guests on special occasions. The lord and his guests sat at the "high table," which stood on a special raised platform called a dais. Grand feasts could start in the morning and last all day.

Small beer

Medieval people normally drank wine or beer, because it was safer than polluted well water. Even children were given weak beer, known as "small beer."

Entertainers

Jesters or fools were among the many entertainers at a feast, along with jugglers, musicians, and traveling actors called **mummers**.

Did you know?

Castle people

A castle was a family home, an army barracks, and an office where the lord's officials collected rents and taxes.

The lord and lady had a staff of clerks who knew how to read, write, and keep accounts. The steward was in charge of the castle staff. Reeves and bailiffs organized the lord's farms and collected rents.

Did you know?

Carve-up

Knights were expected to know how to carve every sort of meat, and the correct word to use for the carving. A deer was *broken*, a swan was *lifted*, a hen was *despoiled*, a duck was *unbraced*, and a peacock was *disfigured*.

Trenchers

The Lord and his honored guests used plates made of silver. Everyone else ate from big slices of stale bread called trenchers. These soaked up all the grease from the food. Used trenchers were given to the poor.

At night the tables and benches were folded away and the servants slept on straw mattresses on the floor.

Canopy

High table

Lord of the castle

Dais

Scraps were thrown on the floor for the dogs.

Medicine

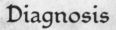
Uroscopy chart

The life of a knight was full of danger. Even when he was not at war, he ran the risk of being seriously injured while jousting or hunting. Wounded knights were sent to surgeons who stopped bleeding by using red-hot irons to cauterize (scorch) a wound. They also sealed wounds with tar. Blood poisoning and a slow death often followed.

Bloodletting

Many diseases were thought to be caused by having too much blood in the body, and the cure was to let some of it out. This could be done by cutting the patient with a knife, or by using leeches (a kind of worm) to suck out the excess blood.

Diagnosis

Since ancient times, doctors have diagnosed illnesses by examining the patient's urine. In medieval plays and stories, the doctor with his specimen bottle is often a figure of fun.

A chart like the one shown above told the doctor how to interpret the urine specimen.

Cutting a hole in the skull (trepanning) was believed to cure various illnesses.

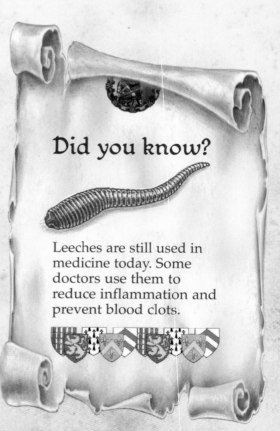

Did you know?

Leeches are still used in medicine today. Some doctors use them to reduce inflammation and prevent blood clots.

Knightly Pastimes

Jesses

Hunting was a knight's favorite way of staying in shape. Deer were hunted on horseback, with dogs, and kings had their own royal deer parks and reserves where no one could hunt without permission.

A favorite form of hunting for both knights and ladies was hawking or falconry, where wild birds of prey were trained to catch other birds.

A hawk in flight. Leather straps called jesses are used to tether the hawk.

A good read

Both knights and ladies enjoyed poems and stories. They would either read these themselves, or have them read or sung, perhaps by a professional musician or "minstrel." Knights could listen to warlike stories about famous heroes such as Roland and Oliver. Ladies might prefer the more romantic tales of King Arthur and his knights. Love songs were popular, and writing them was considered a suitable pastime for a nobleman—even a king.

Wild boar were hunted with hounds and killed with a boar spear. They are very fierce when cornered.

Useful words

accolade a tap on the neck with a sword; part of the knighting ceremony.

arming sword a one-handed sword with a straight, double-edged blade.

buckler a small circular shield.

charge the main design on a coat of arms, such as a lion or a griffin.

chivalry the knightly code of behavior.

courser a swift horse for hunting.

crusade a Christian military expedition to the Middle East.

destrier a warhorse.

dubbing the ceremony of making an esquire into a knight.

esquire a knight's servant, 14–21 years old, who is training to become a knight himself.

falchion a heavy slicing sword with a curved, single-edged blade.

halberd an infantry weapon which consists of a strong spear with an axlike blade.

heraldry the system of badges used to identify knights in battle.

joust a single combat between two knights who ride toward one another with lances.

longsword a two-handed sword with a straight, double-edged blade.

mêlée a mock combat between two teams of knights.

Middle Ages a modern name for the period between 1000 and 1500 CE.

minstrel a professional musician and entertainer; sometimes they were also spies.

page a young servant, 7–14 years old, who hopes to become an esquire.

palfrey a horse for everyday riding.

quintain a target mounted on a swiveling post, used to practice jousting.

ransom money paid by a prisoner or his friends to secure his release; in the Middle Ages this was considered a normal part of warfare.

Saracens the name used by Christians in the Middle Ages to refer to Muslims.

tinctures the standard colors used in heraldry.

tournament a sporting contest consisting of mêlées and jousting.

vigil a night spent in prayer, before a religious festival or before the dubbing ceremony.

Index

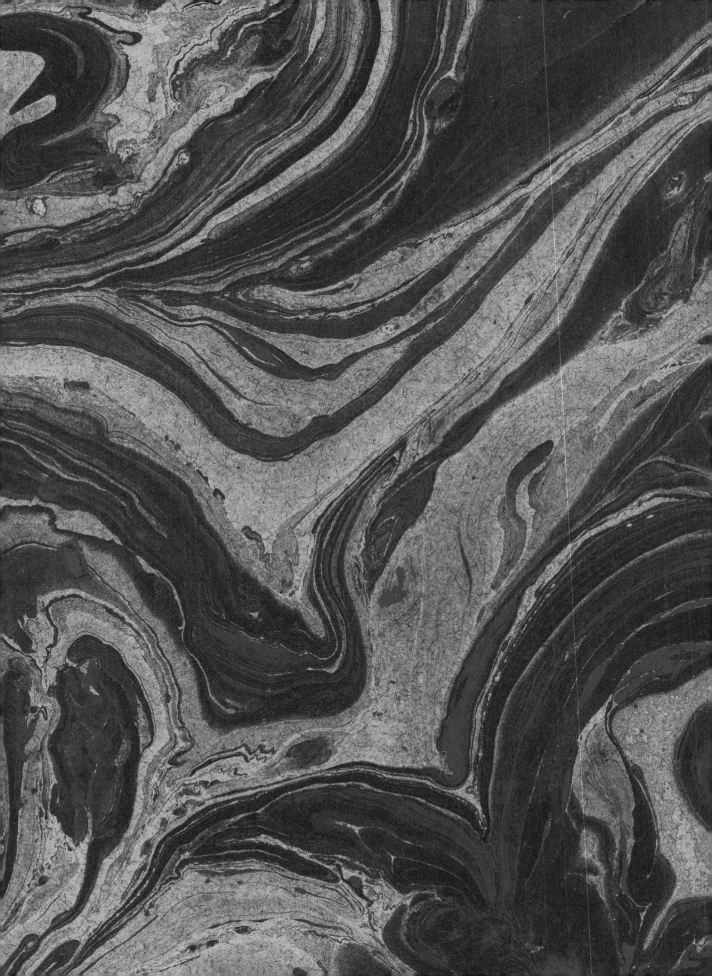